CHESTER
VACATION GUIDE 2023

The Essential and Ultimate Guide to Chester's Hotels, Cuisines, Shopping Tips, Insider's Tips, Top Attractions, History, and Culture

ALFRED FLORES

Copyright © 2023, Alfred Flores

All rights reserved. No part of this publication may be reproduced, distributed, or transmitted in any form or by any means, including photocopying, recording, or other electronic or mechanical methods, without the prior written permission of the publisher, except in the case of brief quotations embodied in critical reviews and certain other noncommercial uses permitted by copyright law.

TABLE OF CONTENTS

INTRODUCTION

CHAPTER ONE:
Getting to Know Chester
   About Chester: Quick Facts and Statistics

CHAPTER TWO:
Planning Your Trip to Chester
   Best Time to Travel
   Visa and Travel Requirements
   How to Get There
   Getting Around
   Accommodation Options
   Travel Insurance

CHAPTER THREE:
Exploring Chester's Top Attractions
   Chester Cathedral
   Chester Rows
   Chester City Walls
   Eastgate Clock

    Chester Zoo

CHAPTER FOUR:
Chester's Hidden Gems
    The Rows Beyond the Main Streets
    Grosvenor Park
    Roman Amphitheatre
    The Watergate
    Chester Ghost Tours

CHAPTER FIVE:
Chester's Historic Sites and Museums
    Grosvenor Museum
    St. John the Baptist's Church
    Roman Gardens
    Dewa Roman Experience
    Chester Castle

CHAPTER SIX:
Experiencing Chester's Cultural Scene
    Chester Music Festival
    Theatre and Performing Arts

Art Galleries and Exhibitions
Literature and Bookshops
Chester Races

CHAPTER SEVEN:
Outdoor Activities in and around Chester
Chester Meadows and River Dee
Delamere Forest
Boating and Kayaking
Cycling and Walking Trails
Golf Courses

CHAPTER EIGHT:
Chester's Culinary Delights
Traditional British Cuisine
Chester's Food Markets
Michelin-Starred Restaurants
Afternoon Tea in Chester
Local Breweries and Pubs

CHAPTER NINE:

Shopping in Chester

   Chester Rows and High Street Shops

   Independent Boutiques and Vintage Stores

   Chester Market

   Antiques and Collectibles

   Souvenirs and Crafts

CHAPTER TEN:

Chester's Nightlife

   Bars and Pubs

   Cocktail Lounges

   Live Music Venues

   Nightclubs and Late-Night Entertainment

   Casino and Gaming

CHAPTER ELEVEN:

Day Trips from Chester

   Liverpool

   Manchester

   The Peak District

The Wirral Peninsula

CHAPTER TWELVE:

Practical Information for Travelers

   Transportation Options

   Money and Currency Exchange

   Language and Cultural Etiquette

   Safety Tips and Emergency Contacts

   Health and Medical Services

CHAPTER THIRTEEN:

Accommodation in Chester

   Hotels and Resorts

   Bed and Breakfasts

   Self-Catering Accommodations

   Boutique and Luxury Stays

   Camping and Caravan Parks

CHAPTER FOURTEEN:

History and Heritage of Chester

   Roman History and Archaeological Sites

   Medieval Chester and Tudor Buildings

   Industrial Revolution in Chester

World War II Heritage

Chester's Famous Residents

CHAPTER FIFTEEN:

Conclusion and Farewell to Chester

CHAPTER SIXTEEN:

Appendix

30 Useful Phrases in English and Local Dialect

Conversion Charts

Packing List for Your Chester Trip

MAP OF CHESTER

INTRODUCTION

Welcome to Chester, a bustling metropolis! Chester, which is located in the center of England, is a place that skillfully combines intriguing culture, a long history, and charming modernity. The *Chester Vacation Guide 2023* is your indispensable travel companion for exploring all that this city has to offer, regardless of whether you're a seasoned traveler or a first-time visitor.

We've included a wealth of useful information in this in-depth guidebook to make sure your trip to Chester is one you won't soon forget. You will immediately become engrossed in this enchanting city's distinctive fusion of modern attractions and ancient Roman heritage.

Chester offers a wide variety of lodging options, and we have carefully chosen the best hotels that suit every need and price range. We have carefully chosen the best solutions to meet your preferences, whether you choose an opulent getaway or a honey boutique hotel. To assist you in selecting the ideal accommodation and ensuring that your trip is one to remember, our guide includes thorough descriptions of features, facilities, and insider advice.

It's always an adventure to explore a city's food scene, and Chester is no exception. This city offers a delicious variety of dining options, ranging from classic British fare to international specialties. Our guide features the best eateries, undiscovered jewels, and neighborhood favorites that will tempt your palate and introduce you to the city's culinary wonders.

As they meander through Chester's picturesque streets, shoppers will discover a shopping paradise. Our guide reveals the top shopping locations to sate your retail needs, whether you're looking for high-end clothing, unusual gifts, or cozy boutiques. To help you make the most of your visit and find gems that represent the city's unique character, we've also included shopping advice and insights.

Without visiting Chester's main attractions, no trip would be complete. Walk around the city's historic walls, admire the famous Chester Cathedral, and learn the mysteries of the Roman amphitheater to fully appreciate the city's fascinating past. You won't miss any of Chester's hidden gems because our guide includes comprehensive information on all the must-see attractions.

We explore the history and culture of the city in order to provide unique insights into Chester's past and present. Explore the city's booming arts sector, learn the history behind its architectural wonders, and catch a peek of the exciting events and festivals that keep this city alive all year long. By illuminating Chester's rich cultural heritage, our tour guide helps you develop a stronger bond with this alluring location.

The *Chester Vacation Guide 2023* is your key to discovering this wonderful city's soul. This handbook is your ideal travel companion for an unforgettable and educational stay in Chester because it is filled with insider advice, useful facts, and engrossing stories. This book includes everything you need, whether you're a history enthusiast, a foodie, an ardent shopper, or just looking for an unforgettable holiday.

So, set out on a voyage of exploration and let the *Chester Vacation Guide 2023* be your dependable travel companion as you explore this unique city's delights. Get ready to experience Chester's magic and make lifelong memories!

CHAPTER ONE:
Getting to Know Chester

About Chester: Quick Facts and Statistics

Here are some quick facts and statistics about Chester:

1. Geographical Overview: Nestled in the northwest of England, Chester is a picturesque city located in the county of Cheshire. Situated on the River Dee, it enjoys a prime location close to the border with Wales. Chester's strategic position has made it an important trading and cultural hub throughout history. The city is approximately 37 miles (60 kilometers) south of Manchester and 24 miles (39 kilometers) southwest of Liverpool, making it easily accessible for travelers from major cities in the region.

2. Population: According to the most recent information, Chester is home to approximately 118,200 people.

3. History: Chester has a lengthy past that goes all the way back to the Roman era. Deva was the name given to it when it was first built as a Roman fort in AD 79. Roman walls and an amphitheater still stand as a testament to the city's Roman past.

4. City Status: Chester, one of the oldest cities in England, has had city status since the Middle Ages.

5. Architecture: Chester is well known for its unusual architectural design. The distinctive

"Rows," two-tiered covered galleries with stores on numerous levels, which date back to the medieval and Tudor eras, are located in the city center.

6. Tourism: Chester is a well-known tourist attraction that draws people from all over the world. It is an interesting city to explore because of its rich history, stunning architecture, and active cultural scene.

7. Economy: The tourism, retail, financial, educational, and healthcare sectors make up part of Chester's diverse economy. In addition, the city is home to a number of significant corporations and a booming retail industry.

8. Education: The University of Chester, which has a sizable student body and provides a variety of academic degrees, is located in Chester.

9. Transportation: Chester has great access to public transit. It boasts an efficient railroad system that connects to significant cities including Liverpool, Manchester, and London. It is simple to navigate around the city as a result of the extensive bus network that serves it.

10. Cultural Events: Throughout the year, Chester hosts a number of cultural events, such as the Chester Music Festival, which features a broad spectrum of musical acts, and the Chester Literature Festival, which honors authors and literature.

11. Climate and Weather: A temperate maritime climate, with warm summers and chilly winters, prevails in Chester. Due to its location near the shore and the impact of the Gulf Stream, the city experiences generally mild weather. Chester's summers are often pleasant, with average highs of 20°C (68°F) and lows of 15°C (59°F). Winters can be chilly, with average temperatures of 2°C (36°F), but they rarely dip below zero. Since it rains every day of the year, it's a good idea to have an umbrella or raincoat with you.

12. History and Culture: Chester has a long, illustrious history that goes back more than 2,000 years. The Romans established the city in AD 79 as a stronghold under the initial name Deva Victrix. The well-preserved city walls and the amphitheater are two particularly visible examples of this old Roman legacy. Chester served as a crucial commerce hub during the medieval era and was well-known for its active markets and stunning buildings.

The classic black-and-white timber-framed buildings that line the city's streets, featuring the characteristic Chester Rows, are a testament to the city's historical significance. These two-tiered medieval galleries are a special aspect of the city that combine dining, shopping, and old-world charm.

Chester has a vibrant cultural scene as well. There are many museums in the city, including the Grosvenor Museum, which explores Chester's Roman past and displays regional artwork and relics. Another cultural treasure that draws visitors is the Chester Cathedral, which has gorgeous Gothic architecture as well as beautiful stained glass windows and a lengthy history.

13. Festivals and Events: Throughout the year, Chester comes to life with exciting festivals and events that provide a wide variety of cultural experiences. The Chester Races, which take place at the storied Chester Racecourse, are one of the most well-known occasions. This prestigious horse racing occasion, which dates back to the early 16th century, attracts people from all across the nation to watch exhilarating races and take pleasure in the festive atmosphere.

The Chester Midsummer Watch Parade is another renowned occasion that happens in June. The magnificent huge figures known as "The Giants" parade through the streets of the city as part of this ancient custom, which dates back to the 13th century. It is a spectacle that highlights Chester's rich legacy and unites the neighborhood in joy.

Chester also holds a number of festivals all year long that cater to various interests, in addition to these major events. With captivating author presentations, readings, and workshops, the Chester Literature Festival honors the written word. Food lovers can savor the Chester Food and Drink Festival, where regional and international delicacies take center stage. Chester regularly hosts events that attract both tourists and residents, from music festivals to Christmas markets.

Chester is a city full of tales and experiences that will have a lasting impact on your journey if you immerse yourself in its vivid tapestry of history, culture, and celebrations.

These quick facts provide a glimpse into the key aspects and characteristics of Chester. Whether you're interested in its Roman history, architectural beauty, or vibrant cultural scene, Chester offers a captivating destination for visitors to explore and enjoy.

CHAPTER TWO:
Planning Your Trip to Chester

Best Time to Travel

Depending on your preferences and the kind of experience you're looking for, there are many best times to visit Chester. When making travel arrangements, keep the following things in mind because the city has something unique to offer at every time of year:

Spring (March to May): Springtime in Chester means pleasant weather and beautiful flowers. Exploring the city's parks and gardens, such Grosvenor Park or the Eastgate Clock Gardens, is a joy during this time. It's a great time to travel peacefully because there aren't as many people as during the summer.

Summer (June to August): During the summer, Chester comes alive and draws a bigger number of visitors. With an average temperature range of 15°C (59°F) to 20°C (68°F), the weather is often nice. The weather is ideal for enjoying boat excursions on the River Dee, seeing the city's outdoor attractions, and attending events and festivals because the days are longer and warmer.

Autumn (September to November): Chester experiences stunning foliage and a quaint ambience in the autumn. Between 10°C (50°F) and 15°C (59°F), the temperatures steadily drop, and the city develops a comfortable atmosphere. A terrific time to stroll along the city walls, visit museums, and explore historical places is now.

Winter (December to February): Chester is a lovely sight in the winter, especially around the holidays. Despite the occasionally frigid weather, which can range from 2°C (36°F) to 8°C (46°F), the city has a welcome and warm vibe. You may stroll around the Christmas markets, attend carol concerts at Chester Cathedral, and admire the city all lit up for the season.

Visa and Travel Requirements

It is crucial to confirm the Chester travel requirements specific to your nationality prior to departure. Depending on your nation of origin, the UK has distinct visa policies. Many nations, including the United States, Canada, Australia, and member states of the European Union, allow tourists to enter the UK for up to six months without a visa. However, to make sure you have the most recent information regarding visa requirements, you should visit the official UK government website or speak with your local embassy or consulate.

Make sure your passport is valid for at least six more months than the length of time you plan to spend in the UK. It's a good idea to include the essential travel documents, such as your passport, visa (if necessary), travel insurance, and any other papers that might be required by immigration officers when you arrive.

How to Get There

Chester is well-connected and simple to get to using a variety of transportation methods:

- By Air: Manchester Airport and Liverpool John Lennon Airport are the two closest major international airports to Chester, each of which is about 25 miles (40 kilometers) from Chester. Both airports provide handy options for travelers by providing both domestic and international flights. You can take a rail, bus, or cab from the airports to get to Chester.

- By Train: Chester has great rail accessibility, with direct train service available from the UK's largest cities. Chester Railway Station, the city's train station, is conveniently positioned and offers easy access to the city center. Regular trains run between London Euston and Chester, with a two-hour average travel time.

- By Car: Chester is conveniently reachable by road if you want to drive. The M53 and M56 highways offer direct access to the city, making it well-connected to the country's highway system. There are a number of parking lots across the city, including ones close to the city center and popular attractions.

- By Bus: National and local bus services connect Chester with its nearby towns and cities. They run to and from Chester. A key hub for bus transit is the Chester Bus Exchange, which is close to the city center.

Once you've arrived in Chester, you can get around the city and get where you need to go using public transit choices like buses and taxis.

Planning your transportation in advance should take into account your preferences and the Chester destinations you want to see. Think about things like pricing, convenience, and how close your lodging is to different transportation hubs.

Getting Around

Getting around Chester is simple once you get there because of its small size and well-connected transit network. Here are several methods of transportation:

- Walking: Chester is a pedestrian-friendly city, and many of its sights to see, stores to visit, and restaurants are all close by. You can fully appreciate the city's historic neighborhoods, attractive landscapes, and distinctive architecture by strolling around on foot.

- Public Transportation: Chester has a well-organized system of buses and trains for getting around town. Local bus services are run by Stagecoach, and they provide convenient routes around the city and its surroundings. You can also go to adjacent cities and towns by train, which has a center at the Chester Railway Station.

- Taxis: In Chester, taxis are easily accessible and a practical means of transportation, particularly for shorter trips or when you have a lot of luggage. Taxis can be requested on the street, through a local taxi company, or through ride-hailing applications.

- Bicycles: Cycling is a common means of transportation in Chester, a city that encourages it. You may explore the city at your own speed while taking advantage of the beautiful scenery and designated cycling pathways by renting a bicycle from one of the many businesses that offer hourly or daily rentals.

- Car Rental: Chester offers car rental services if you prefer the option of having your own vehicle. Renting a car gives you the freedom to explore the neighborhood and its attractions at your own pace. Rental businesses have a variety of vehicles to meet your preferences. It's crucial to keep in mind that parking in the city center may be scarce and that some attractions can have particular parking requirements.

Accommodation Options

Chester provides a variety of lodging choices to accommodate all tastes and price ranges. There are several options available in the city, whether you're looking for luxury, boutique, or affordable lodging. Popular choices comprise:

- Hotels: Chester has a wide selection of hotels, from opulent five-star inns to cozy mid-range properties and affordable lodgings. You can easily access the city's top attractions, restaurants, and retail areas if you choose to stay in the city center.

- Bed and Breakfasts (B&Bs): B&Bs offer a comfortable and homey ambiance, frequently run by hospitable owners who can impart local knowledge and insights. They are a popular option for people looking for a more individualized experience and a filling breakfast to start the day.

- Guesthouses: Chester's guesthouses provide a cozy and cost-effective lodging choice. They are an excellent option for tourists on a tight budget because they frequently offer a variety of services, such as individual rooms and shared facilities.

- Self-Catering Apartments: Chester offers self-catering apartments if you'd prefer a more independent and roomy lodging alternative. Having a kitchen in these completely furnished apartments allows you to prepare meals and experience living away from home.

Travel Insurance

A crucial component of organizing your trip to Chester is travel insurance. In the event of unforeseen occurrences like trip cancellations, medical problems, or missing luggage, it offers financial protection and peace of mind. Here are some important things to think about:

- Coverage: Make sure your travel insurance policy provides coverage for medical costs, trip cancellations or interruptions, personal liability, and lost or stolen property. It's a good idea to find out if the policy covers activities or needs unique to your vacation, such pre-existing medical issues or adventure sports.

- Policy Details: Read the insurance terms and conditions carefully to understand the coverage, as well as any exclusions or limits, before purchasing the policy. Pay close attention to the claims procedure, deductibles, and coverage restrictions. To locate the insurance plan that best meets your needs, it is advisable to select a trustworthy insurance company and examine several coverage options.

- Duration: Make sure your travel insurance covers the entire duration of your trip, from the moment you leave your home until your return. If you plan to engage in any activities before or after your time in Chester, ensure that your coverage extends to those periods as well.

- Additional Coverage: Consider any additional coverage you might require in light of your unique situation. Check your insurance policy to see if it covers activities like participating in adventure sports, for instance. You might want to think about getting additional coverage for your important possessions.

- Policy Documents: While traveling, keep a copy of your travel insurance policy documentation on hand. These documents should include emergency contact information. Additionally, discussing these specifics with a dependable family member or friend is a good idea.

Examine your current insurance policies, such as your health and homeowner's insurance, to see whether they provide any coverage for travel before buying travel insurance. Check your credit card to see whether it offers travel insurance benefits as some credit cards do.

You may travel to Chester with confidence and peace of mind by getting the right travel insurance. This will allow you to take full advantage of your vacation.

You can plan your trip to Chester with ease, ensuring a hassle-free and enjoyable experience by taking into account the best time to visit, reviewing visa and travel requirements, understanding the transportation options, exploring various accommodation options based on your preferences, and securing comprehensive travel insurance.

CHAPTER THREE:
Exploring Chester's Top Attractions

Chester Cathedral

A must-see site in the city is Chester Cathedral, a beautiful architectural masterpiece. Its beginnings can be found in 1092, the year a Benedictine abbey was built there. The Cathedral Church of Christ and the Blessed Virgin Mary, the contemporary Gothic-style cathedral, was built over several centuries and features beautiful craftsmanship and complex embellishments.

The cathedral's grandeur and tranquility will enthrall you as soon as you enter. Admire the grand organ, stunning stained glass windows, and sweeping ceilings. Enjoy the serenity and sense of history that are all around you for a minute.

The Lady Chapel, the Chapter House with its medieval wall murals, and the renowned choir stalls are some of the cathedral's highlights. Atop the cathedral tower, visitors may get stunning 360-degree views of the city and its surroundings.

Chester Rows

The Chester Rows are a distinctive element that distinguishes the city from others. Along some of the city's major thoroughfares, such as Watergate Street, Eastgate Street, Northgate Street, and Bridge Street, are these two-tiered, covered walkways. The Rows, a magnificent architectural wonder from the Middle Ages, feature stores, boutiques, and eateries on the ground floor and covered walkways and further stores above.

It feels like time has stopped when you walk along the Rows. The rows themselves offer a unique shopping experience, and the black-and-white timber-framed buildings ooze charm and character. You'll come across a variety of independent stores, stylish boutiques, cozy cafes, and classic pubs as you explore.

The Rows provide a fascinating synthesis of culture, retail therapy, and culinary delights. Take your time exploring these eerie passageways, exploring the one-of-a-kind stores, and soaking in the energetic atmosphere of this unique sight.

Chester City Walls

The historic city walls of Chester are among its most recognizable and well-maintained landmarks. These walls, which the Romans built in the first century AD and which enclose the city center, offer a fascinating look into Chester's illustrious past. As you stroll along the walls, you can take in the city's layout, architecture, and harmonious fusion of the old and new.

A leisurely stroll along the walls' whole circuit, which is about 2 miles (3.2 kilometers) long, will take you past significant landmarks. From a number of locations, including Eastgate, Northgate, and Watergate, among others, you can approach the walls. You'll pass through historical sites like the Roman amphitheater, the

Eastgate Clock, and the lovely Chester Racecourse as you walk around the walls.

The walls offer a peaceful retreat from the busy city below. You can take your time to take in the scenery, stop at the sporadic towers along the way, and learn about the legends engraved into the old stones. Being able to connect with Chester's Roman and medieval past while strolling the city walls makes it a special way to discover Chester.

Eastgate Clock

A well-known landmark and an iconic representation of Chester is the Eastgate Clock. This elaborate clock, which is located over the Eastgate entrance to the city, was built to honor Queen Victoria's Diamond Jubilee, which was unveiled in 1899. It is one of the most often photographed clocks in the world and a well-liked gathering spot for both locals and tourists.

The elaborate clock's design includes Gothic-style arches, decorative ironwork, and a bronze sculpture of a winged lion sitting atop the building. It not only keeps time but also gives the city's skyline a touch of elegance. This famous timepiece, which serves as a reminder of Chester's rich history and legacy, will catch your attention as you walk down Eastgate Street.

The Eastgate Clock is a focal point for events and celebrations all year long in addition to being a visual joy. It has been the site of innumerable parades, gatherings, and festivities, earning it the status of a symbol of pride and community. When you visit Chester, be sure to take a picture with this wonderful clock.

Chester Zoo

Chester Zoo, a well-known attraction that is not far from the city center, guarantees an unforgettable experience for animal enthusiasts of all ages. It is one of the biggest and busiest zoos in the UK, with over 35,000 animals from more than 500 different species living there.

At Chester Zoo, we put a lot of focus on education, conservation, and animal care. The animals are in a cozy and stimulating environment thanks to the large enclosures and realistic habitats. The Islands, which displays Southeast Asian fauna, and the spectacular Realm of the Red Ape, which is home to orangutans and other primates, are two themed zones where visitors can travel.

The zoo provides a variety of fun and instructive activities. You may take part in daily feeding and chat sessions with the animals, see engaging animal performances, and even get a behind-the-scenes look with VIP interactions. The variety of fauna at Chester Zoo is simply amazing, ranging from regal big cats to lively penguins.

Chester Zoo is devoted to global conservation activities in addition to its fascinating animal exhibits. It delivers educational programs to spread awareness of the significance of biodiversity and environmental sustainability and actively supports research and conservation efforts.

The Chester Zoo promises an amazing day of wildlife encounters, educational activities, and a chance to help support crucial conservation efforts. It's a must-see destination that will provide you priceless memories and a newfound appreciation for nature.

You may learn more about Chester's extensive history and architectural wonders by exploring the city's finest attractions, including the beautiful Chester Cathedral, the distinctive Rows, the old city walls, the Eastgate Clock, and Chester Zoo. Each site offers a distinctive experience that highlights Chester's allure, history, and cultural importance. When you embark on this exploratory voyage, you'll develop a greater understanding of the city's distinct personality and eternal beauty.

CHAPTER FOUR:
Chester's Hidden Gems

Chester is home to various hidden treasures that provide unique experiences outside of the main tourist destinations, and it has a rich history and attractive streets. These undiscovered jewels offer a chance to learn more about the history, scenery, and lesser-known attractions of the city. Let's look at a few of Chester's undiscovered gems:

The Rows Beyond the Main Streets

While Eastgate Street and Watergate Street's Rows are well-known and humming with bustle, exploring farther out exposes unexpected gems. Discover the quieter, more private areas of the city by exploring the lesser-known Rows including Commonhall Street, Bridge Street, and Lower Bridge Street.

These obscure Rows frequently provide a more genuine and regional experience. These dark, winding lanes are home to hidden cafes, art galleries, and boutique stores. You can avoid the crowds and savor Chester's beauty on a quieter level by strolling through these secret Rows.

Grosvenor Park

Grosvenor Park is a secret haven of peace and unspoiled beauty, tucked away on the banks of the River Dee. Over 20 acres in size, this Victorian park provides a tranquil escape from the busy city core. Grosvenor Park offers a tranquil place for relaxation and outdoor activities with its well-kept grass, vibrant flower beds, and established trees.

Discover a peaceful area to have a picnic while taking a leisurely stroll through the park's twisting trails and admiring the Victorian iron bridge's ornate ironwork. The park also has a kid-focused play area and a miniature railway that's great for a family outing.

Shakespeare plays and other theatrical works are frequently performed outside at Grosvenor Park during the summer. The park is a great place for both theater aficionados and those who enjoy the outdoors thanks to these performances, which give it a touch of cultural energy.

Roman Amphitheatre

Visit the Roman Amphitheatre, a hidden jewel that provides a window into the city's Roman past, and uncover Chester's ancient history. One of the biggest Roman amphitheaters in Britain is located here, and it is close to Chester Castle just outside the city walls.

Built in the first century AD, the amphitheater could hold up to 7,000 spectators who came to watch thrilling gladiatorial fights and other public performances. In order to appreciate the splendor of the events that formerly took place there, one might visit the amphitheater's ruins today.

Stroll over the stone walls that originally surrounded the audience area, take a seat in the main arena, and take in the ruins of the tunnels that once housed the gladiators and their companion animals. Informational panels and displays offer details on the background and significance of the location.

You may connect with Chester's Roman heritage and develop a deeper understanding of the city's historical past by visiting the Roman Amphitheatre. It's a little-known treasure that reveals more of Chester's past than the more well-known sights.

The Watergate

Another undiscovered treasure in Chester that provides a window into the city's medieval past is The Watergate. At the westernmost point of the city walls, this historic gate leads to the magnificent Chester Racecourse and serves as a reminder of Chester's long history.

Originally constructed in the 14th century, the Watergate has seen numerous alterations and augmentations over the years. It has a tower and a characteristic archway that were formerly a part of the city's defenses. You'll feel like you've stepped back in time when you approach the Watergate because of its overwhelming presence.

The Watergate is notable not only for its historical significance but also for its breathtaking views of the River Dee and the surroundings. Reach the tower's summit by climbing the stairs, where you can take in expansive views of the river, the city, and the racetrack. It's the ideal location for photographers and others looking for a serene vantage point to take in Chester's splendor.

Chester Ghost Tours

Chester Ghost Tours offer an exciting and eerie experience for individuals who are captivated by the paranormal and the stories of the unexplained. These guided tours take you on a spooky tour of the city's paranormally active streets while sharing ghost stories, urban legends, and sinister secrets that dwell in the shadows.

The ghost tours explore Chester's most haunted spots and dig into its terrifying history under the guidance of skilled and entertaining experts. As night sets, you'll stroll through dimly lit streets, hear chilling tales, and see alleged haunted locations. To provide an unforgettable experience, the guides skilfully meld history, folklore, and dramatic storytelling.

Whether you believe in ghosts or not, Chester's ghost tours provide a fascinating look into its past and present. They give you the chance to experience the city in a new way, learn about its sinister legends, and take in the eerie atmosphere that surrounds these haunted locations.

Chester's ghost tours cater to a variety of interests and age groups, offering everything from family-friendly excursions to more intense encounters for thrill-seekers. Joining a ghost tour is not only a thrilling way to see the city, but it's also a chance to hear fascinating tales and get a glimpse into the enigmatic side of Chester's past.

You can add a layer of investigation and surprises to your vacation by learning about Chester's little-known attractions including the Rows, Grosvenor Park, the Roman Amphitheatre, the Watergate, and going on a ghost tour. You can discover untold tales, peaceful havens, and antiquated relics at these off-the-beaten-path destinations, which add to the rich fabric of Chester's legacy.

CHAPTER FIVE:
Chester's Historic Sites and Museums

Chester is a historical city with a plethora of museums and historical landmarks that provide unique insights into its past. Visitors can fully immerse themselves in Chester's rich past and cultural significance by touring these landmarks and institutions. Let's examine some of Chester's illustrious monuments and museums:

Grosvenor Museum

The Grosvenor Museum, which lies in the center of the city, is home to a vast collection of artifacts and displays that highlight Chester's history from Roman times to the present. The impressive Grade II-listed structure that houses the museum is named for the powerful

Grosvenor family, who made a substantial contribution to the growth of the city.

The museum's significant collections include artwork, social history exhibits, and archaeological discoveries. With displays of Roman relics, including beautiful mosaics and items from the neighboring Roman fortification of Deva Victrix, you can dig into Chester's Roman past. The museum also focuses on Chester's industrial past and highlights the medieval and Victorian eras of the city.

The Grosvenor Museum also holds transient exhibitions that focus on particular facets of Chester's history and culture in addition to its permanent holdings. The museum attracts history buffs and families alike with its interactive exhibits, kid-friendly activities, and educational guided tours.

St. John the Baptist's Church

On the intersection of Vicar's Lane, St. John the Baptist's Church is a 12th-century architectural marvel. The stunning stained glass windows, elaborate woodwork, and historical landmarks of this Grade I listed building are well known. It is considered one of Chester's finest examples of medieval construction.

As soon as you enter St. John the Baptist's Church, you'll notice its serene atmosphere and exquisite architectural elements. Admire the grand columns, lofty nave, and stunning stained glass windows that depict biblical tales. Take some time to go around the side chapels where you can find elaborate stone carvings and old memorials.

The church has a tower as well, which affords stunning views of the cityscape and the surroundings. To fully appreciate the city's architecture, especially that of the surrounding cathedral and the River Dee, climb the tower.

Roman Gardens

The Roman Gardens, a haven of calm just outside the city walls, honor Chester's Roman past. Built on the site of a Roman fort, this attractively landscaped park contains a variety of antiquity and artifacts from the time the Romans ruled Britain.

Roman constructions are still visible as you stroll through the Roman Gardens, including pieces of the Roman city walls and the ruins of a Roman hypocaust (underfloor heating system). The well-known Nemesis shrine, which was found during 19th-century excavations, is also housed in the park.

Visitors can connect with Chester's Roman past while unwinding and reflecting in the tranquility of the Roman Gardens. The meticulously kept gardens, colorful flower beds, and peaceful setting provide for a beautiful backdrop for a leisurely stroll or picnic.

Dewa Roman Experience

Roman Chester, also known as Deva Victrix, is the setting of the interesting interactive museum known as the Dewa Roman Experience. This distinguished attraction, which is situated on the former site of a Roman stronghold, presents a rare chance to understand life during the Roman conquest of Britain.

Roman-themed tour guides will welcome you as you enter the Dewa Roman Experience and take you through a number of replica buildings. You may put yourself in the shoes of a Roman citizen, engage with the exhibitions, and take part in practical activities thanks to the immersive exhibits.

Explore the archaeological finds made at the site, learn about Roman daily life, and become familiar with Roman crafting methods. The opportunity to observe a Roman soldier's practice and even put on real Roman armor is one of the experience's highlights.

The Dewa Roman Experience offers an enthralling fusion of entertainment, archaeology, and history. It presents a vivid depiction of Roman Chester life and a distinctive viewpoint on the city's antiquity. This interactive museum is a must-see in Chester whether you're a history buff, a family with kids, or just interested in the Roman era.

Chester Castle

The impressive Chester Castle, which is close to the city's heart, is a reminder of Chester's role in the Middle Ages' military development. Although a large portion of the castle is off limits to visitors, its surroundings and exterior are interesting to explore.

William the Conqueror initially constructed the castle in the 11th century as a defensive fortress and administrative hub. It underwent numerous alterations over the years and functioned as a royal home, a prison, and a military barracks.

The Agricola Tower is Chester Castle's most noticeable feature right now. This medieval tower, which bears the name of the Roman general Agricola, provides insight into the castle's past. It houses the Cheshire Military Museum, which exhibits a variety of relics, uniforms, and weapons while highlighting the area's military past.

You can still see the old walls and gates as you go through the castle grounds, which once housed historic defenses. Due to its lovely setting close to the River Dee, the castle is a popular site for leisurely strolls and photo ops.

Chester Castle's interior is not accessible to the general public, but the outside and the Cheshire Military Museum provide fascinating insights into Chester's military history. History buffs and others interested in medieval architecture will find the castle to be interesting due to its imposing appearance and historical relevance.

The Grosvenor Museum, St. John the Baptist's Church, the Roman Gardens, the Dewa Roman Experience, and Chester Castle are just a few of the historic locations and museums that provide an enthralling look into Chester's past. These sites provide you a better knowledge of the city's rich history and cultural importance, whether you're interested in archaeology, architecture, or social history. You can unravel Chester's history and appreciate its unique role in the history of Britain by visiting these historical landmarks and museums, which is like traveling back in time.

CHAPTER SIX:
Experiencing Chester's Cultural Scene

Chester has a thriving cultural environment with a wide variety of artistic and entertainment opportunities. Chester's cultural landscape offers something for everyone to enjoy, from concerts to plays, exhibitions to literary events, and thrilling horse racing. Let's look at the different facets of Chester's cultural scene:

Chester Music Festival

The Chester Music Festival is an annual celebration of classical music that draws well-known performers and music lovers from all over the world. The festival's schedule includes symphonic concerts, chamber music recitals, and recitals performed in renowned locations including Chester Cathedral and the old Town Hall.

The festival features a range of musical styles, including choral performances, symphonies, and contemporary composers. It offers a stage to both well-known performers and up-and-coming musicians, fostering a lively environment that appeals to music fans of all ages.

You may immerse yourself in the allure of classical music at the Chester Music Festival and take in the beauty and power of live performances in breathtaking locations.

Theatre and Performing Arts

Chester is home to a number of theaters and performance spaces that provide a wide variety of theatrical productions, dance performances, comedy events, and more. The theaters in the city, such as the Storyhouse and the Forum Studio Theatre, present a varied schedule of plays, musicals, and avant-garde performances.

The Storyhouse is a cultural center that comprises a theater, cinema, library, and café, housed in a gorgeously restored art deco movie theater. It offers a diverse lineup of performances, from West End shows to modern creations, and it also hosts community activities and workshops.

Chester cultivates local talent through amateur theater organizations and public performances in addition to professional shows. Chester theater performances offer a chance to admire the performing arts and give back to the neighborhood arts scene.

Art Galleries and Exhibitions

Chester's art galleries and shows feature a variety of conventional and contemporary artistic styles and media. There are many galleries in the city, including the Grosvenor Museum Art Gallery, which regularly hosts exhibitions of local and foreign art.

Chester has a thriving contemporary art culture, and places like the Chester Art Centre and the Artichoke Gallery regularly feature new and known artists' works. The exhibitions, talks by artists, and workshops held by these galleries frequently give art lovers the chance to interact with the creative process.

You can explore various artistic expressions, find new talents, and participate in stimulating discussions about art and culture by going to art galleries and exhibitions in Chester.

Literature and Bookshops

With numerous bookshops, literary festivals, and literary events held throughout the year, Chester boasts a lively literary scene. The city's bookshops provide a warm and welcoming atmosphere for book enthusiasts while offering a variety of volumes, from bestsellers to specialist categories.

Each year, the Chester Literature Festival brings together renowned writers, poets, and speakers for thought-provoking lectures, panel discussions, and workshops. The event encourages a love of literature and storytelling while celebrating the written word.

You can immerse yourself in the world of books, find new authors, and interact with like-minded people who share a passion for literature by exploring Chester's bookshops and going to literary events.

Chester Races

A significant event in the city's cultural calendar is Chester Races. Race fans and socialites alike flock to the storied Chester Racecourse, a horse racing venue close to the city's heart, for a number of renowned horse racing occasions every year.

A fantastic experience is attending a race day at Chester Races. The racecourse's distinctive layout, which includes its short straight and tight corners, produces a cozy yet exciting ambiance. You may watch thrilling horse races, make bets, and revel in the thrill of rooting for your favorite horse.

Chester Racecourse features a variety of social and entertainment events in addition to the races, including live music concerts, food festivals, and family-friendly activities. It offers a full day of entertainment, with options for excellent dining, champagne in the Champagne Garden, or just taking in the lively ambiance of the racetrack.

Experiences of Chester's cultural offerings, whether they be through music festivals, theatrical productions, art exhibits, literary events, or horse racing at Chester Races, are comprehensive and engaging. It enables you to engage with many artistic mediums, support regional artists, and contribute to Chester's lively and enriching cultural landscape.

CHAPTER SEVEN:
Outdoor Activities in and around Chester

For those who love the outdoors and are looking for adventure, Chester and the surrounding areas have a wealth of outdoor activities. There are several options to appreciate nature, from serene woodlands to exhilarating water activities and scenic river bank walks. Let's look at some of the most popular outdoor pursuits in and near Chester:

Chester Meadows and River Dee

Just beyond the municipal limits, Chester Meadows is a lovely area of vegetation that runs beside the River Dee's meandering course. This picturesque location makes the ideal backdrop for leisurely strolls, picnics, and relaxation.

You may wander down the riverbank while soaking in the peaceful environment and beautiful views of the surrounding landscape and the water. The meadows are a popular location for bird watching because they are home to many different bird species.

Take a leisurely boat ride along the River Dee for a more immersive experience, where you can unwind and take in the breathtaking surroundings. Alternatively, you might try your hand at fishing because the river is well recognized for having plenty of salmon and trout.

Delamere Forest

Delamere Forest, which is close to Chester, provides a tranquil haven and a variety of outdoor pursuits. This vast forest offers chances for biking, strolling, wildlife viewing, and other outdoor activities, making it ideal for nature lovers and other outdoor enthusiasts.

The broad network of trails in Delamere Forest can accommodate hikers of all skill levels and tastes. There are paths for all skill levels, whether you prefer a leisurely stroll or a harder hike. While exploring the forest, you might see deer, squirrels, and various bird species because it is home to a wide variety of flora and animals.

Delamere Forest also has bicycle trails, including family-friendly and mountain biking-specific routes. For an active day amidst nature, you can rent bikes on-site or bring your own.

Boating and Kayaking

Boating and kayaking enthusiasts have wonderful chances on the River Dee and neighboring lakes. There are options for all levels of experience, whether you choose a calm paddle or an exhilarating adventure.

You can take a relaxing and beautiful adventure by renting a rowboat or a pedal boat to explore the River Dee's calm waters. Alternatively, if you're looking for more adventure, paddling a kayak or a canoe down the river or on one of the nearby lakes is an exhilarating experience that lets you explore the rivers and take in the beautiful surroundings.

Cycling and Walking Trails

A network of biking and walking trails is available in Chester and the surrounding countryside, catering to all levels and tastes. You can explore the city's ancient streets and sights on foot because it is small and convenient for getting around on foot.

Numerous pathways crisscross the scenic Cheshire countryside outside the city. For instance, the Sandstone Trail offers a picturesque stroll through lovely trees and along the sandstone ridge, offering breath-taking views of the surroundings.

For those who enjoy cycling, there are designated routes like the Chester Millennium Greenway and the Cheshire Cycleway that take you through quaint towns, gorgeous landscapes, and along paths free from traffic.

Golf Courses

Chester and its neighboring environs provide a variety of golf courses that are suitable for players of all ability levels. Golfers can enjoy their favorite sport amidst breathtaking scenery on championship courses as well as more laid-back and accessible options.

The golf courses in and near Chester provide a variety of challenges and amenities, whether you're an expert golfer or a novice looking to perfect your swing. You can take pleasure in the game while admiring the surrounding area's natural beauty.

By participating in outdoor activities in and around Chester, you may discover the beautiful landscapes, get in touch with nature, and experience thrilling adventures. There are outdoor activities to suit every interest and degree of fitness, whether you decide to stroll through the lovely Chester Meadows, set off on a biking or walking track, delve into the peaceful Delamere Forest, or indulge in boating and kayaking on the River Dee.

These outdoor activities offer a chance to get away from the city's bustle, take in some fresh air, and take in the scenic surroundings of Chester. The outdoor activities in and around Chester offer a wide variety of possibilities to sate your outdoor needs, whether you're looking for adventure, leisure, or a chance to connect with nature.

Therefore, Chester and its surrounds provide a wide range of outdoor activities to enjoy, whether you're strolling along the River Dee, admiring the serenity of Delamere Forest, kayaking on the water, touring the countryside on foot or by bike, or playing a round of golf. Enjoy the beauty of nature, spend time outside, and make memories that will last a lifetime in this alluring area.

CHAPTER EIGHT:
Chester's Culinary Delights

Chester has a vast variety of gastronomic pleasures that cater to a variety of tastes and inclinations, making it a heaven for food enthusiasts. The city has a thriving food scene that will tempt your taste buds with everything from traditional British food to cosmopolitan delicacies. Let's look at some of Chester's culinary offerings' highlights:

Traditional British Cuisine

Chester is the ideal location to savor authentic British cuisine. The area is renowned for its quaint bars and eateries serving time-honored fare like fish and chips, substantial pies, Sunday roasts, and traditional afternoon tea.

At one of the many fish and chip shops strewn throughout the city, you may indulge in the pleasures of freshly battered fish and crispy golden chips paired with mushy peas and tartar sauce. Try a traditional pie, like steak and ale or chicken and leek, with creamy mashed potatoes and rich gravy for a hearty and full lunch.

In Chester, afternoon tea is another delectable treat. Enjoy a range of finger sandwiches, freshly baked scones with jam and clotted cream, and a variety of exquisite pastries and cakes, all served with a warm pot of tea. This distinctly British delight is available in many tearooms and hotels throughout the city, allowing you to unwind and enjoy an afternoon of indulgence.

Chester's Food Markets

Chester is home to thriving food markets that highlight the local cuisine and vegetables. The lively Chester Market in the center of the city is home to a variety of stalls selling fresh fruit, artisanal bread, regional cheeses, gourmet meats, and other items.

For food lovers, the market is a gold mine because it offers the chance to try regional specialties, buy fresh products, and interact with local merchants. Street food, ethnic cuisine, specialty coffees, and sweet desserts are all available. Food lovers who want to learn more about the regional culinary scene should definitely visit the market because of its lively atmosphere and wide variety of goods.

Michelin-Starred Restaurants

For those seeking fine dining, Chester is home to a few Michelin-starred establishments that provide remarkable experiences. These restaurants exhibit the culinary prowess of outstanding chefs and produce delicious dishes using the finest seasonal and local ingredients.

A Michelin-starred meal in Chester guarantees a culinary adventure with unique taste combinations, exquisite presentation, and first-rate service. The menus frequently include inventive dishes that push the limits of conventional flavors, making for a distinctive and unforgettable eating experience.

These eateries offer the ideal atmosphere for celebratory events, special occasions, or just a night of indulgence. Due to their popularity and the small number of available tables, reservations are advised.

Chester offers a wide variety of international cuisines to satisfy all preferences in addition to classic British cuisine, vibrant food markets, and Michelin-starred restaurants. Without leaving the city, you may go on a global gastronomic journey that includes Indian curry houses, Mediterranean bistros, Asian fusion restaurants, and Italian trattorias.

Afternoon Tea in Chester

Chester is well known for offering exquisite afternoon tea experiences that offer a truly British tradition with a dash of sophistication. The city's many tearooms, hotels, and cafes offer the ideal backdrop for indulging in this cherished culinary tradition.

In Chester, afternoon tea often consists of a tier-stacked stand with a variety of finger sandwiches, freshly baked scones with clotted cream and jam, and an alluring range of exquisite pastries and cakes. With a range of flavors and mixes to pick from, the tea itself is a key component, assuring a perfect combination with the sweet and savory delicacies.

Many places in Chester elevate the traditional practice of afternoon tea by putting themed versions or original spins on it. You could find themed teas inspired by the seasons or special occasions, or champagne afternoon teas that include a glass of bubbly to go with the delectable nibbles.

The experience promises a refined and unwinding ambiance whether you choose a classic afternoon tea or something with a unique twist. Indulge in delightful conversation, take in the opulent surroundings, and appreciate the delicacies of this beloved British institution.

Local Breweries and Pubs

A number of regional brewers that make a variety of craft beers and ales call Chester home. Beer fans must visit the city's breweries and sample their products.

You can stop by microbreweries and taprooms, like the well-known Chester Brewhouse & Kitchen, where you can take a guided tour, observe the brewing process firsthand, and sample a variety of their handcrafted beers.

Many of these breweries provide a warm and welcoming ambiance that enables you to unwind with friends or other beer enthusiasts while savoring a pint or two of their best brews.

Chester is well-known for its breweries as well as its quaint taverns, some of which have been welcoming visitors for decades. These charming, old-fashioned bars are the perfect place to unwind with a drink, whether it's a local brew, a great whiskey, or a light cocktail. The classic furnishings seen in the pubs, such as exposed beams, open fireplaces, and cozy corners, add to their attractiveness.

To fully experience Chester's beer culture, drink a variety of flavors, and interact with passionate brewers and pub owners, visit local breweries and establishments. It's an opportunity to try out new brews, appreciate the skill and hard work that goes into brewing them, and take pleasure in the friendly environment that comes with sharing a pint with friends.

You can appreciate the complex flavors, take in the distinctive food culture, and unearth culinary gems by discovering Chester's gastronomic wonders. Chester offers a delectable variety of culinary options that are sure to please even the most discriminating palate, whether you're a fan of traditional British fare, eager to explore the local food markets, looking for an upscale dining experience, delightful afternoon tea, exploring the local brewing scene, or enjoying a pint in a historic pub.

CHAPTER NINE:
Shopping in Chester

Chester is a shopper's paradise with an extensive selection of stores to suit all tastes and inclinations. The city is a paradise for anyone seeking retail therapy, from the distinctive architecture of the Chester Rows to the bustling main street stores, independent boutiques, and vibrant markets. Let's investigate the various facets of shopping in Chester:

Chester Rows and High Street Shops

The Rows is one of Chester's commercial district's most recognizable characteristics. These unusual two-tiered covered galleries from the Middle Ages are crammed with a variety of stores, cafes, and eateries. With their distinctive architectural elements and black and white timbered facades, The Rows offer a beautiful and ethereal backdrop for shopping.

Numerous high street stores, including well-known brands and independent merchants, are located in The Rows. Numerous fashion boutiques, beauty salons, jewelry stores, gift shops, and other establishments are available. You can find hidden treasures and have a shopping experience that is genuinely exclusive to Chester by exploring the Rows.

Chester features a bustling high street with well-known chain businesses and department stores in addition to the Rows. You can indulge in some shopping therapy at this area's many fashion, beauty, home décor, and electronics stores.

Independent Boutiques and Vintage Stores

Chester has a booming independent boutique culture for individuals looking for something a little more distinctive and different. There are numerous independent fashion boutiques, lifestyle shops, and specialty businesses spread out all throughout the city that sell an unusual assortment of clothing, accessories, and home goods.

These shops offer carefully chosen selections, frequently showcasing regional designers and artisans. You may support small companies, get one-of-a-kind items, and personalize your home or wardrobe by shopping at these boutiques.

Additionally, Chester is home to a number of vintage and retro shops where you can find undiscovered artifacts from bygone times. These shops allow you to embrace nostalgia and discover one-of-a-kind items with a backstory by offering a carefully chosen range of vintage clothing, accessories, and home goods.

Chester Market

Foodies and shoppers alike congregate in the thriving Chester Market. The market, which is housed in a historic structure in the center of the city, has a wide variety of stalls selling local crafts, fresh vegetables, and other products.

You can purchase fresh produce at Chester Market, peruse a selection of cheeses, meats, and baked products, or find one-of-a-kind handmade goods and artwork. The market also has food vendors where you may sample cuisines from around the world or indulge in regional specialties.

The market is a must-visit for anyone looking for a distinctive shopping experience or in search of fresh and locally sourced products because of its bustling environment, friendly traders, and different offerings.

Antiques and Collectibles

For lovers and collectors of antiquities, Chester is a gold mine. There are numerous antique stores and dealers in the city that sell a variety of rare and expensive things. Chester's antique shops are a thrill to browse, whether you're an experienced collector or just enjoy the elegance of vintage items.

There are antique shops that specialize in a variety of items, including books, jewelry, pottery, furniture, and much more. These places frequently feature carefully curated collections, each of which has a unique narrative and historical relevance. You can find hidden treasures, locate unusual items, and give your collection or home decor some history and character by browsing around antique shops.

The owners of many of Chester's antique stores are informed and enthusiastic about what they have to offer. They can help you make informed judgments and deepen your understanding of antiques by sharing information on the history and provenance of the objects.

Souvenirs and Crafts

Chester has a lot to offer in terms of souvenirs and handcrafted goods from the area. You can find quaint gift shops and craft boutiques all across the city that feature the creations of regional makers.

These stores are brimming with one-of-a-kind, handcrafted goods that capture the spirit of Chester and its surroundings. There are numerous souvenirs and crafts available, ranging from handcrafted pottery, textiles, and jewelry to locally created artwork and photography.

You can bring home a reminder of your visit to Chester while also supporting regional artists and aiding in the preservation of traditional crafts and practices by buying souvenirs and handmade items from these independent shops.

Chester's bustling markets, like the Chester Market and sporadic craft fairs, provide opportunities to find locally manufactured crafts and artisanal goods in addition to the shops. These markets frequently have booths selling handcrafted items including jewelry, paintings, textiles, pottery, and jewelry.

Chester offers a beautiful fusion of the old and the new when it comes to shopping, from perusing the quaint Rows and high street retailers to finding independent boutiques and vintage shops. Chester offers a rich and varied retail scene that appeals to all tastes and inclinations, whether you're looking for the newest fashion trends, one-of-a-kind pieces, locally sourced goods, a distinctive vintage item, or a handcrafted souvenir.

CHAPTER TEN:
Chester's Nightlife

Chester comes to life at night with a dynamic and varied nightlife culture that appeals to a variety of interests and inclinations. Chester offers a variety of entertainment options, whether you want a quiet evening at a traditional pub, an elegant cocktail experience, or a night of live music and dancing. Let's investigate the various facets of Chester's nightlife:

Bars and Pubs

There are numerous bars and pubs in Chester that provide something for everyone. You may find a spot to fit your tastes anywhere, from quaint, traditional pubs to hip, sophisticated bars.

In Chester, traditional pubs frequently include historic decor that includes exposed beams, open fireplaces, and a variety of beers, ales, and ciders. These places offer a warm and laid-back setting that is ideal for sharing a pint with friends or taking in the neighborhood vibe.

On the other side, Chester also has modern bars that provide a more up-to-date and fashionable experience. These establishments frequently provide a wide variety of craft beers, cutting-edge cocktails, and a vast array of wines and spirits. These places are well-liked options for hanging out and having a good time because of their stylish interiors and energetic ambiance.

Cocktail Lounges

Chester has a number of cocktail bars that provide beautifully made beverages and an upscale ambience for those looking for a sophisticated and polished evening. These places frequently have talented mixologists that make imaginative and distinctive drinks with premium spirits and seasonal ingredients.

Chester's cocktail lounges offer the ideal atmosphere for indulging in inventive cocktails and taking advantage of a more upmarket and exclusive experience. These lounges provide a variety of options to please your palate, whether you prefer traditional cocktails or cutting-edge concoctions. Enjoy the comfort of beautifully crafted cocktails, the flavors of soft sitting, and the company of friends or loved ones in a chic environment.

Live Music Venues

Chester's live music venues, where you can enjoy a variety of performances from local musicians to well-known performers, enliven the city's evening scene. Whether you prefer rock, jazz, folk, or pop music, you can discover places that feature a range of genres.

Chester has a variety of live music venues, from small acoustic settings to huge concert halls, catering to all tastes. You can attend performances by local bands, solo artists, or even visiting performers, giving both well-known groups and up-and-coming musicians a stage.

The nightlife in Chester is lively and dynamic because of the numerous clubs and pubs that organize live music events in addition to the dedicated music venues. You may take in the social atmosphere of the venue while taking in the excitement of a live performance.

By going to a live music event in Chester, you may learn about new musicians, support your community's music scene, and experience the excitement of live performances in a warm, lively setting.

Nightclubs and Late-Night Entertainment

Chester offers a variety of late-night entertainment options for people looking for a fun and exciting night out. These places offer a lively environment where you may dance, mingle, and have a good time.

Nightclubs in the city play a variety of music, from top songs to electronic dance music, to suit varied preferences. Numerous clubs hold themed nights, special events, and guest DJs to create a dynamic and thrilling atmosphere. These venues produce an exciting atmosphere that keeps the party going into the early hours thanks to cutting-edge sound systems, mood lighting, and skilled DJs.

Chester provides a range of late-night entertainment alternatives in addition to nightclubs, including comedy clubs, cabaret shows, and live concerts. These places offer an alternate night out for individuals seeking something different, mixing comedy, entertainment, and interactive experiences.

Casino and Gaming

Chester boasts a casino that provides an interesting gaming experience if you're feeling lucky or seeking for a thrill. The casino offers a variety of activities, such as blackjack, poker, roulette, and slot machines, where you may test your luck and take pleasure in the thrill of gambling.

Whether you're a seasoned pro or a beginner wishing to try your luck, the casino offers a friendly setting with knowledgeable personnel who can help and direct you through the games. Additionally, a lot of casinos include bars, restaurants, and live entertainment, giving patrons a full range of entertainment options.

In Chester's casino, you may mingle with others, put your talents to the test, and spend the evening playing games and having fun.

Chester's nightlife has a range of options to suit different tastes, whether you're searching for an enjoyable live music experience, a classy cocktail event, or a casual evening at a classic pub. Because Chester has such a wide variety of clubs, pubs, cocktail lounges, and live music venues, there is usually something going on after dark. Chester offers a dynamic and bustling nightlife that appeals to a variety of tastes and interests, whether you prefer the energetic atmosphere of nightclubs, the sophisticated ambiance of cocktail bars, the excitement of live music, the thrill of gaming, or a combination of these experiences.

CHAPTER ELEVEN:
Day Trips from Chester

Chester is a great starting point for exploring adjacent locations because of its central location. There are several day trip alternatives that let you explore the region's great diversity, from dynamic cities to breathtaking natural scenery. Following are three well-liked day-trip locations from Chester:

Liverpool

Liverpool, a thriving and culturally diverse city with a long maritime heritage, is only a short drive from Chester. Liverpool has a wide range of attractions and activities because it is the birthplace of The Beatles and the location of renowned buildings like the Albert Dock and the iconic Liver Building.

Visit the UNESCO World Heritage-listed waterfront, home to museums, art galleries, and exhibitions, to learn more about the city's interesting past. While the Museum of Liverpool highlights the history and culture of the city, The Beatles Story Museum offers a thorough trip through the life and music of the Fab Four.

Liverpool is also well known for having a flourishing music culture, with several live music venues showcasing a range of performers. You can attend a concert at the storied Cavern Club, where The Beatles first attained renown, or see a performance at the Philharmonic Hall or Echo Arena.

Manchester

Manchester is a bustling city well-known for its industrial past, cultural attractions, and energetic vibe, and it makes for another wonderful day trip from Chester. Manchester provides a variety of world-class shopping, historical architecture, cultural attractions, and an active music and arts scene.

Visit the Museum of Science and Industry or go on a tour of the Manchester Ship Canal to learn more about the city's rich industrial past. Both the Manchester Art Gallery and the Whitworth Art Gallery feature a wide variety of modern and historic works of art for art lovers.

Visits to Old Trafford, the storied home of Manchester United, or the Etihad Stadium, where Manchester City plays, are sure to please football lovers. Both stadiums offer guided tours that give visitors an understanding of the clubs' accomplishments and history.

Manchester is also renowned for its amazing shopping, with the Northern Quarter's busy streets showcasing a variety of independent boutiques, vintage shops, and hip cafés. Another feature of the city is its eclectic food scene, which offers a wide variety of international cuisines and cutting-edge dining options.

The Snowdonia National Park and North Wales: A day excursion to North Wales and Snowdonia National Park is essential for anyone who enjoys the outdoors and the natural world. You can lose yourself in the breathtaking natural scenery of mountains, lakes, and charming villages within a short drive of Chester.

With Mount Snowdon being the highest mountain in Wales, the Snowdonia National Park offers stunning landscapes. The park offers hiking, mountain biking, and beautiful drives as outdoor pursuits. For expansive views of the surroundings, ride the Snowdon Mountain Railway to Mount Snowdon's peak.

Another well-liked vacation spot in North Wales is the beach town of Llandudno, which is well-known for its Victorian beauty. Visit the Great Orme, a limestone headland that is home to a wildlife preserve and an old copper mine, or simply unwind on the sandy beaches.

Conwy Castle is a magnificent medieval fortification and a UNESCO World Heritage site that provides a window into Wales' extensive history. You can enjoy expansive views of the town and the estuary while taking a guided tour of the castle's towers, walls, and chambers.

The Peak District

The Peak District National Park, which is only a short distance east of Chester, is another fantastic day travel option. The Peak District, well-known for its beautiful scenery and outdoor pursuits, provides the ideal getaway into nature.

Rolling hills, untamed moorlands, deep valleys, and picture-perfect communities define the park. It's the perfect location for outdoor activities including hiking, biking, rock climbing, and exploring. You have a variety of trails and paths to select from, so you may go for a leisurely stroll or a more challenging hike.

One of the most iconic landmarks in the Peak District is Mam Tor, a hill with panoramic views of the surrounding area. You can climb to the summit and take in the breathtaking vistas of the peaks and valleys.

The picturesque communities located inside the park, such Bakewell and Castleton, provide visitors a glimpse of country life in the old-fashioned sense of the word. You can stroll the streets, explore historic sites, look around your neighborhood's stores, and savor regional specialties like the renowned Bakewell tart.

For both lovers of the outdoors and thrill seekers of adventure, the Peak District makes a wonderful day trip destination.

The Wirral Peninsula

The Wirral Peninsula, located across the River Mersey from Liverpool, makes for a lovely day trip from Chester. This idyllic region is well-known for its breathtaking coastline, quaint towns, and distinctive attractions.

The Wirral Peninsula is home to lovely beaches including West Kirby and New Brighton where you can take a leisurely stroll down the shore, unwind on the sand, or even try your hand at water sports. Explore the fascinating marine life in the rock pools or take in panoramic views of the Liverpool skyline.

One of the Wirral Peninsula's must-see locations is Port Sunlight Village. The founders of the Lever Brothers soap company (now Unilever), the Lever Brothers, constructed this model hamlet in the late 19th century. The village is home to lovely architecture, exquisitely planted gardens, and a museum that sheds light on the region's past.

Wirral Country Park provides a tranquil area for walking, cycling, and birdwatching for nature lovers. This vast park includes ponds, meadows, and forests, offering a range of wildlife with habitats.

On their way back from the Wirral Peninsula, history buffs might also want to stop by Chester, which is just a short distance across the River Dee.

You may enjoy the diversity of the area by taking day trips from Chester to Liverpool, Manchester, North Wales, the Peak District, and the Wirral Peninsula. These day trip destinations give you the opportunity to experience the diverse landscapes and cultural offerings of the region, resulting in a well-rounded and enriching travel experience, whether you're exploring the cultural offerings of the cities, submerging yourself in natural beauty, or learning about the region's history.

CHAPTER TWELVE:
Practical Information for Travelers

When traveling to Chester, it's critical to be knowledgeable about useful tips that can improve your trip's efficiency and enjoyment. Here are some important factors to think about:

Transportation Options

Excellent transit alternatives are available in Chester, making it simple to move around the city and explore the surroundings:

1. Public Transportation: The public transportation network in Chester is well-connected. The city has buses that run through the heart of the city and allow quick access to a number of attractions. Additionally,

the Chester train station offers connections to important UK cities like Liverpool and Manchester, making day trips easy.

2. Walking: The city core of Chester is small and accessible by foot. You can appreciate the city's historic beauty and find hidden jewels while exploring on foot. With well-kept sidewalks and designated pedestrian areas, the city is pedestrian-friendly.

3. Taxis and Rideshares: Rideshares are also widely accessible in Chester, and you can either find one at a designated taxi stand or hail one on the street. There are also ridesharing services like Uber that offer a practical and frequently less expensive alternative to conventional taxis.

Money and Currency Exchange

The following are some crucial specifics about money and currency exchange in Chester:

1. Currency: The British Pound Sterling (£) is the unit of exchange in the United Kingdom. Make sure you have enough cash or a frequently used debit or credit card.

2. Currency Exchange: Chester has a number of banks and places where you may exchange your money into British Pounds. Additionally, there are numerous ATMs located throughout the city where you can use your debit or credit card to withdraw cash. To avoid any problems with card usage, it is advisable to let your bank or card provider know about your vacation intentions.

3. Credit Cards: The majority of Chester's businesses, including hotels, restaurants, and stores, accept major credit cards including Visa and Mastercard. Nevertheless, it's wise to always have some cash on hand for minor purchases or locations that might not accept cards.

Language and Cultural Etiquette

The language most often used in Chester is English. But understanding cultural etiquette can aid you in navigating relationships and demonstrating respect for the regional traditions:

1. Greetings and Politeness: A simple "hello" or "good morning/afternoon" is appropriate when meeting someone for the first time. Saying "please" and "thank you" when making requests or accepting assistance is customary.

2. Tipping: Tipping is usual in Chester, and if you had good treatment, you should typically leave a tip of between 10% and 15% of the entire bill in restaurants, cafes, and bars. To prevent leaving two tips, it is wise to check the bill at some businesses because they could include a service charge.

3. Cultural Sensitivity: Chester visitors must respect the diversity of all cultures. Be aware of regional traditions, customs, and religious practices. When visiting holy places or going to formal gatherings, it is best to dress modestly.

4. Queuing: Waiting in line is a major matter in the UK. Follow the line and wait for your turn if you're in a public area or business. Cutting people in front of you is rude.

Safety Tips and Emergency Contacts

1. General Security: Chester is a safe city, however it's always wise to take security measures. Keep an eye out for potential hazards, especially at night or in crowded settings. Keep an eye on your possessions and keep expensive goods hidden when not in use. It's best to stick to well-lit, well-traveled paths while you're out on your own, especially at night.

2. Emergency Contacts: Dial 999 for police, ambulance, or fire services in the event of an emergency. In the UK, this is the standard emergency phone number. You can phone 101 to request non-emergency police assistance if you need help but it's not an emergency.

3. Travel Insurance: Having comprehensive travel insurance that covers medical costs, trip cancellation or interruption, and personal possessions is highly advised. Make sure you always carry a copy of your insurance policy and emergency contact information.

Health and Medical Services

1. Medical Facilities: If you require medical attention, Chester boasts a number of medical facilities, including hospitals, clinics, and pharmacies. The Countess of Chester Hospital, a large medical facility inside the city, is the closest significant hospital to Chester.

2. European Health Insurance Card (EHIC): If you are a citizen of an EEA nation or of Switzerland, it is advisable to travel with a

current EHIC, which allows you essential medical care at the same cost as local residents. Please take note that the new UK Global Health Insurance Card (GHIC), which offers comparable healthcare benefits, is taking the role of the EHIC.

3. Pharmacies: Chester is home to many pharmacies, often known as chemists. They offer over-the-counter drugs, counsel on minor ailments, and, if necessary, can point you in the direction of suitable medical services. To find a nearby drugstore, look for the green "Pharmacy" sign.

4. COVID-19 Considerations: Keep up with the most recent COVID-19 regulations and rules announced by the local authorities. Follow social seclusion guidelines, use face masks when

necessary, and maintain proper cleanliness, including frequent handwashing. It's a good idea to research any particular rules and regulations before your trip.

It's crucial to note that the information above is subject to change, so it's advised to stay current by contacting your embassy or consulate before your travel, local authorities, or official websites.

You can feel at ease during your visit to Chester by becoming familiar with the available modes of transportation, the currency conversion, cultural etiquette, safety advice, emergency contacts, and health services. You can also travel Chester with ease and respect local customs. These useful tips will improve your travel experience and enable you to get the most out of your time in this wonderful city.

CHAPTER THIRTEEN: Accommodation in Chester

You can choose from a number of lodging alternatives to suit your needs and budget while making travel plans to Chester. The city offers a variety of options to enhance your stay, whether you're seeking opulent hotels, quaint bed and breakfasts, or self-catering lodging. Here is a list of the several lodging options available in Chester:

Hotels and Resorts

Chester is home to a wide range of hotels and resorts that may accommodate different preferences and budgets. You'll discover options that fit your needs, from comfortable three-star lodgings to opulent five-star places.

Chester's luxury hotels offer first-rate amenities, flawless service, and opulent surroundings. They frequently have spa services, upscale eating options, workout centers, and luxurious rooms or suites. When you stay at these places, you may treat yourself to a high level of comfort and have a wonderful experience while you're there.

Mid-range hotels in Chester offer a balance between comfort and affordability. They provide comfortable rooms, essential amenities, and sometimes include additional features such as on-site dining, swimming pools, or fitness centers. These hotels provide a comfortable stay without breaking the bank.

Budget hotels or budget-friendly chains are also available in Chester, providing clean and comfortable rooms at a more affordable price point. These lodgings are perfect for tourists on a tight budget who desire convenience and good value.

Bed and Breakfasts

Consider booking a room at a lovely Chester bed and breakfast for a more individualized and intimate experience. These lodgings offer cozy, comfortable rooms, frequently with warm and inviting owners as hosts. Typically smaller in size, bed and breakfasts offer a cozy and private setting that encourages greater connection with the hosts and other guests.

Every morning you can anticipate a great breakfast that frequently includes homemade or local food. You may enhance the charm and character of your stay in Chester by staying at one of the bed and breakfasts housed inside a historic structure.

Self-Catering Accommodations

Chester offers a variety of rooms to suit your needs if you like the adaptability and independence of self-catering. Serviced flats, cottages, townhouses, or vacation homes with individual living areas and fully functional kitchens are examples of self-catering accommodations.

These lodgings are perfect for families or groups who want their own kitchens and lots of space to unwind. They frequently include numerous bedrooms, living spaces, and extra amenities like gardens or private parking. Self-catering lodgings provide you more control over your daily schedule and let you create a "home away from home" environment while you're abroad.

Chester lodging can be reserved directly with the hotel or through internet travel agencies that provide a range of choices and customer ratings. When selecting your lodging, make sure it fits your demands by taking into account your preferences, spending capacity, and preferred location.

Boutique and Luxury Stays

Chester has a variety of boutique hotels and luxury accommodations if you're seeking for a distinctive and upscale lodging experience. These places offer a fusion of luxury, refinement, and individualized attention to make your stay memorable and indulgent.

Chester's boutique hotels are renowned for their distinct personalities and are frequently located in old or well designed buildings. Because they have fewer rooms available, the ambiance is more intimate and exclusive. In order to deliver an authentically opulent experience, boutique hotels carefully manage their design and decor to represent a specific theme or concept.

Chester offers a variety of options for luxurious accommodations, including manor homes, country estates, and five-star hotels. These lodgings offer large, tastefully decorated rooms or suites, top-notch amenities, and top-notch service. They frequently have upscale restaurants, spas, or fitness centers on-site, as well as attractively landscaped gardens or grounds.

You can immerse yourself in elegant surroundings, get first-rate service, and enjoy the finer things in life while visiting Chester by selecting a boutique or luxury accommodation.

Camping and Caravan Parks

Chester provides camping and caravan sites in picturesque areas for individuals who seek a closer connection to nature or are traveling in a campervan or caravan.

Tents, camper vans, or motorhomes can stay in amenities at camping grounds in and near Chester. These locations frequently feature amenities including shower and toilet facilities, electric hookups, and shared kitchen and gathering areas. Camping in Chester enables you to take in the tranquility of the outdoors while staying close to the city's services and attractions.

Chester offers caravan sites for those who are taking their own mobile home. These parks offer the required amenities, such as electricity, water hookups, and garbage disposal points, for designated pitches. Additionally, some campgrounds could provide facilities like playgrounds, stores, or recreation areas.

You can have a more adaptable and outdoor-focused experience while staying at a campground or caravan park, with the opportunity to explore the local area and activities at your own speed.

It's a good idea to make reservations in advance when selecting a boutique, luxury, camping, or caravan in Chester, especially during busy times or for special occasions. This guarantees availability and enables you to book the kind of lodging that fits your needs and travel schedule.

Chester offers a variety of options to suit different preferences, whether you prefer an opulent hotel, a cozy bed and breakfast, self-catering lodging, boutique hotels and luxury stays for an indulgent experience, or camping and caravan parks for those seeking a closer connection to nature. Choosing the ideal lodging improves your whole experience and enables you to unwind and relax after visiting the city's attractions.

CHAPTER FOURTEEN:
History and Heritage of Chester

Chester is a historical city with a storied past spanning several centuries. Chester offers a fascinating voyage through time, from its Roman origins to its medieval and Tudor buildings, industrial revolution legacy, World War II heritage, and association with renowned residents. Let's explore each facet of Chester's past and culture:

Roman History and Archaeological Sites

Chester was a prominent castle and hamlet of the Roman Empire, called in those days as Deva. Its establishment in AD 79 gave the Romans a strategic foothold from which to rule Britannia's northwest.

The Chester Roman Amphitheatre is the city's most well-known Roman building. Gladiatorial matches and other events used to take place at this archaeological site, which is in good condition. Visitors can now wander around the amphitheater's ruins and imagine the ancient performances that once took place there.

The Chester Roman Gardens, which are close to the city walls, are another impressive Roman structure. You can see remnants of Roman structures here, such as pieces of the Roman hypocaust system that heated the adjoining Roman baths centrally.

Medieval Chester and Tudor Buildings

Chester is home to a plethora of medieval and Tudor buildings, which speaks to the significance of this thriving medieval city. The Chester Cathedral, which was initially constructed as a Benedictine abbey in the tenth century, is the most recognizable representation of medieval Chester. It is a must-see location for history buffs due to its spectacular Gothic architecture, exquisite stained glass windows, and medieval carvings.

Chester's city walls are yet another noteworthy example of medieval architecture. These beautifully restored walls enclose the city's core and provide picturesque views of the area's landmarks. As you tour the Eastgate Clock, one of Chester's most recognizable buildings, you get an insight into the city's medieval past while strolling around the city walls.

A distinctive architectural element from the Middle Ages is Chester's Rows. Considered to be the oldest retail galleries in Europe, these two-tiered covered galleries host stores. With their characteristic black and white timbered facades, they exhibit a fusion of medieval and Tudor structures.

Industrial Revolution in Chester

Chester saw substantial economic expansion and modernization during the Industrial Revolution. Among other industries, the city was involved in the production of textiles, pottery, and ships.

The Chester Canal, built to move commodities between Chester and the industrial hubs of the Midlands, is one prominent legacy of the Industrial Revolution. The canal still exists in certain places today, and you may take a leisurely stroll along its towpath to admire the scenery and discover its historical significance.

World War II Heritage

Chester served as a key military and strategic hub during World War II. Several military training facilities, including the Western Approaches Tactical Unit (WATU) and the RAF Sealand airfield, were located in the city. In the midst of the conflict, WATU, which was based in the Town Hall's basement, was crucial to the development of naval strategy.

Explore the Chester Military Museum, which displays items from many eras, including World War II, and highlights the city's military past.

Chester's Famous Residents

Famous people who made an impact on history have lived in Chester. John Speed, an English cartographer well-known for his maps of the United Kingdom and other regions of the world, is one of the most well-known locals. His 1611 publication, "The Theatre of the Empire of Great Britaine," is an important historical document.

Rupert Brooke, a well-known author and poet, also resided in Chester while attending the University of Cambridge. One of his well-known poems is "The Old Vicarage, Grantchester".

Investigating Chester's history and traditions provides an engrossing window into the city's past. Chester has a rich tapestry of historical significance that immerses visitors in its enthralling narrative, from its Roman origins and medieval architecture to its legacy from the Industrial Revolution, World War II past, and association with renowned residents.

CHAPTER FIFTEEN:
Conclusion and Farewell to Chester

It's time to say goodbye to this fascinating city as your tour of Chester's history, culture, attractions, and experiences comes to a close. Chester has given you a genuinely unforgettable visit because of its Roman heritage, medieval charm, industrial past, and rich cultural tapestry.

You have been in awe of Chester's famous sights all throughout your journey, including the magnificent Chester Cathedral, the charming Rows, and the old Roman amphitheater. You have strolled alongside the ancient city walls while picturing the legends enshrined in their ancient stones. You've immersed yourself in the local culture by going to concerts, watching plays, and admiring the exciting art galleries and exhibitions.

You've been able to learn about the various landscapes, cultures, and attractions that surround Chester thanks to your day travels to surrounding locations including Liverpool, Manchester, North Wales, the Peak District, and the Wirral Peninsula. Every place you go, from the crowded city streets to the serene serenity of nature, adds its own special flavor to your travels.

Your taste buds have been tantalized by Chester's delectable cuisine, which ranges from classic British fare to decadent afternoon teas and regional beers at the city's lovely pubs and cafes. In the shopping areas, you may find souvenirs and indulge in retail therapy thanks to a variety of high street brands, independent boutiques, markets, and special finds.

As you leave Chester, you bring with you memories of the city's historic sites, the friendliness of its residents, and the educational opportunities that made your stay genuinely memorable. You now have a deeper grasp of this extraordinary city because of the information you've learned about its Roman background, medieval legacy, industrial significance, and World War II heritage.

Chester has extended a warm welcome and invited you to appreciate its traditions, history, and culture. As you say goodbye, you take a piece of Chester with you, permanently woven into the tapestry of your recollections. It has made an enduring impression on your trip journey.

May Chester's inspiration never fade, stoke your desire to explore, and ignite a passion for culture, history, and the unforgettable experiences that travel can offer. Chester, I'll miss you until we cross paths again on fresh adventures.

CHAPTER SIXTEEN: Appendix

In this appendix, you will find some useful information and tools to assist you during your Chester trip. These tools will improve your experience and make your vacation more enjoyable. They range from helpful phrases to conversion charts and a packing list.

30 Useful Phrases in English and Local Dialect

In order to assist you navigate conversations and engage with locals, here are 30 useful English phrases and a few words in the regional dialect:

English:

1. Hello/Hi - A common greeting.

2. Thank you - Expressing gratitude.

3. Excuse me - Used to get someone's attention or apologize.

4. Please - A polite word to use when making a request.

5. Can you help me? - Asking for assistance.

6. Where is...? - Seeking directions.

7. How much does it cost? - Inquiring about the price.

8. I'm sorry - Apologizing for a mistake.

9. Do you speak English? - Asking if someone can communicate in English.

10. What is your name? - Getting to know someone's name.

11. I don't understand - Indicating confusion.

12. Could you repeat that, please? - Asking someone to repeat what they said.

13. How do I get to...? - Asking for directions to a specific place.

14. I need a doctor - Seeking medical assistance.

15. Can I have the bill, please? - Requesting the check at a restaurant.

16. Where is the nearest ATM? - Inquiring about the location of the closest ATM.

17. Do you have Wi-Fi? - Asking if there is internet access available.

18. Can you recommend a good restaurant? - Seeking a restaurant recommendation.

19. What time does it open/close? - Inquiring about opening and closing times.

20. Is there a pharmacy nearby? - Asking for the location of a nearby pharmacy.

21. Is this seat taken? - Asking if a seat is already occupied.

22. Can you help me with my luggage? - Requesting assistance with luggage.

23. May I take a photo? - Asking for permission to take a photograph.

24. Cheers! - A common toast when raising a glass.

25. Have a nice day! - Wishing someone a pleasant day.

26. Where can I buy tickets? - Inquiring about ticket purchase locations.

27. Can you recommend any attractions to visit? - Seeking recommendations for places to visit.

28. What time does the train/bus leave? - Inquiring about departure times.

29. Is there a restroom nearby? - Asking for the location of a restroom.

30. Goodbye - Saying farewell.

Local Dialect (Cheshire):

1. Ay up - A greeting similar to "hello."

2. Ta - Short for "thank you."

3. Owt - Means "anything."

4. Nowt - Means "nothing."

5. Scran - Food or a meal.

6. Mardy - Someone who is moody or sulky.

7. Snap - Food or a packed lunch.

8. Chuffed - Delighted or pleased.

9. Mither - To bother or annoy.

10. Latch - To close or shut.

Remember, these phrases are just a starting point, and locals will appreciate your effort to communicate and connect with them.

Conversion Charts

When traveling to a new country, having conversion charts for currency, temperature, and measurement units can be helpful. Here are some commonly used conversion charts for your convenience:

Currency Conversion:

1 British Pound (GBP) is approximately equal to:

- 1.17 Euros (EUR)

- 1.37 US Dollars (USD)

- 1.96 Australian Dollars (AUD)

- 1.66 Canadian Dollars (CAD)

- 1.78 Swiss Francs (CHF)

- 153.67 Japanese Yen (JPY)

- 11.14 Chinese Yuan (CNY)

Please note that exchange rates fluctuate and may vary slightly depending on where you exchange your currency. It's always advisable to check the latest exchange rates before your trip or consult with a local bank or currency exchange office for the most accurate and up-to-date information.

This currency conversion chart will assist you in estimating the value of your currency when exchanging it for British Pounds during your visit to Chester.

Temperature Conversion:

°F to °C: [(°F - 32) / 1.8]

°C to °F: [(°C * 1.8) + 32]

Measurement Conversion:

1 inch = 2.54 centimeters

1 mile = 1.609 kilometers

1 pound (lb) = 0.454 kilograms

1 fluid ounce (fl oz) = 29.574 milliliters

These conversion charts will assist you in quickly converting between different units of measurement during your stay in Chester.

Packing List for Your Chester Trip

To ensure you have everything you need for a comfortable stay, here's a suggested packing list for your Chester trip:

Clothing:

- Weather-appropriate clothing (considering the season)
- Comfortable walking shoes
- Raincoat or umbrella
- Hat and sunglasses
- Swimwear (if visiting during summer)

Travel Essentials:

- Valid passport and necessary travel documents
- Travel insurance information
- Local currency (British Pounds) and/or debit/credit cards

- Power adapters and chargers for your electronic devices
- Portable charger for your mobile phone
- Language translation app or phrasebook

Health and Safety:
- Prescription medications (if applicable)
- Basic first aid kit
- Personal hygiene products
- Sunscreen and insect repellent
- Any necessary medical documents or prescriptions

Miscellaneous:
- Travel guidebook or map of Chester
- Camera or smartphone for capturing memories
- Travel locks for securing your belongings
- Day bag or backpack for carrying essentials during sightseeing

- Snacks and a refillable water bottle for on-the-go refreshments

It's important to customize this packing list based on your personal preferences, the duration of your trip, and the specific activities you plan to engage in while in Chester.

By utilizing these useful phrases, conversion charts, and packing list, you'll be well-prepared to make the most of your visit to Chester. Enjoy your trip and embrace the history, culture, and beauty that this remarkable city has to offer!

MAP OF CHESTER

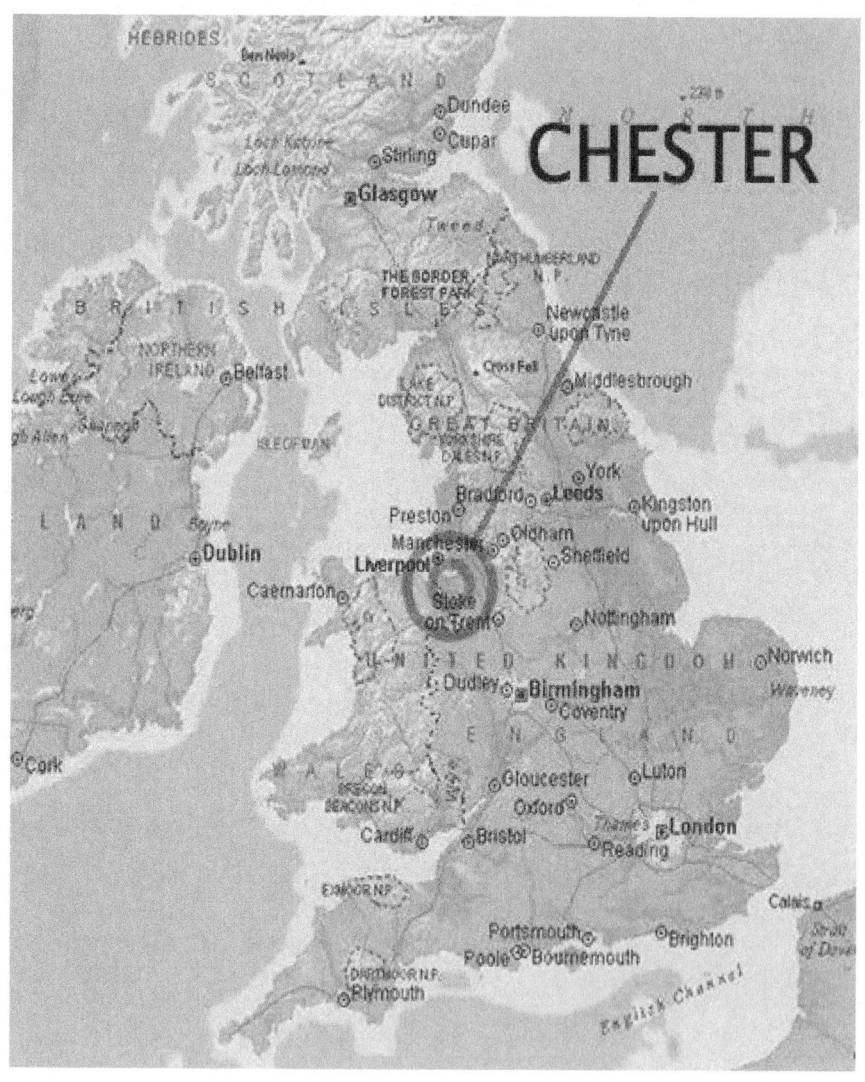

Printed in Great Britain
by Amazon